Johnny Carson

a blind date

Illustrated by

Whitney
Darrow, Jr.

DOUBLEDAY AND COMPANY, INC.
GARDEN CITY, NEW YORK

Special Thanks to
Walter Kempley and Edwin Weinberger
for their contributions
to the text of this book.

Publishing Consultant: J. P. Tarcher

misery is...

Misery is:

explaining the birds and bees to your
young son and then overhearing him
tell the little girl next door,
Guess what, you're going to have a bee..."

misery is:

not having any money when
the representative comes to your house
selling Mafia cookies.

misery is:

laughing at your husband because
he can't get into his old army uniform
and then you can't get into
your old maternity dress.

Whitney Darrow, Jr.

misery is:

going on your honeymoon and having
the motel employees toss a
"Welcome Back" party for your bride.

misery is...

going to a temperance meeting
and your breath
sets off the sprinkler system.

Misery is:

wearing a topless bathing suit and
having a man walk up to you and say:
"Nice day today, sir."

misery is:

a girl asking if she can come up
to your place and
you still live with your mother.

Misery is:

sneaking in your house
at four in the morning
and finding your wife
sneaking out.

Misery

bursting in on your wife in the
arms of the milkman...
when you owe money to the cleaner.

finding out your daughter's screen test
has just been sold as
an Army training film.

getting an acting role in "Peyton Place"
and discovering it's the part of
a bedridden missionary.

putting on your underarm deodorant
and it turns out to be
your dog's flea and tick spray.

going to a formal affair and having
a moth ball fall out of your pants.

climbing your daughter's jungle gym
and having to call the fire department
to help you down.

misery is:

buying a sports car and
discovering that your bucket
is bigger than the seat bucket.

misery is;

a girl asking you to accompany her
to Niagara Falls for a big thrill
and then discovering she means
going over it in a barrel.

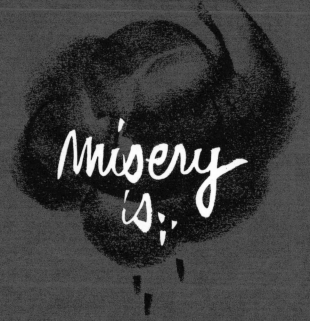

misery is:

an undertaker trying to look sad
at a $5,000 funeral.

going on your honeymoon and seeing
your bride kneel beside the bed and say,
"Now I lay me down to sleep."

misery is:

going to a topless bar the same day
you had your eyes dilated.

misery is;

cooking an exotic French dish
for five hours and then having
your husband put catsup on it.

misery is;

being served with a paternity suit
during your first speech as president
of the Planned Parenthood Association.

misery is...

your secretary saying LBJ is on the telephone and then finding out it's the subscription department of the Louisiana Breeder's Journal.

misery is:

your waist measurement keeping even with your age.

a mother-in-law who tries
to commit suicide but fails…
and runs up a big gas bill.

kissing your wife good night
and having her
put your lip up in a hair curler.

finding that your daughter is engaged
to a man of the cloth and
he turns out to be
the Imperial Eagle of the KKK.

going out with a sweater girl
and discovering
she's more sweater than girl.

a sexy girl dropping her handkerchief
and when you bend over to pick it up,
your toupee falls off.

complimenting your boss's wife
on her patterned stockings and
finding out
she isn't wearing stockings.

misery is:

going to a costume ball
as a bubble dancer
and finding out your date is going
as a porcupine.

misery is:

having your handsome boss ask you
to work late at the office...
then finding out he wants you
to work late at the office.

misery is:

finding out your wife received
312 valentines from the
Tijuana Cab Drivers Association.

misery is:

when you ask your doctor
if he can cure you
and he asks to be paid in advance.

misery is:

chasing your secretary,
then catching her and being
too winded to do anything about it.

misery is;

learning the pitter patter of
little feet around the house is
because your wife is seeing a midget.

Misery is:

finding out your daughter's boy friend
just bought an amplifier for his guitar.

Whitney Darrow Jr.

misery

going to work and discovering
you're wearing your seven-year-old son's
jockey shorts.

discovering your deodorant
is giving you bad breath.

going up to the attic and reading your
wife's love letters and seeing that
they're all dated last week.

showing off in your new Cadillac and
crashing into a Volkswagen driven by
your internal revenue agent.

having your wife hurt in a
hunting accident because
she looks so much like a moose.

being invited to an American Legion
stag film and finding out it's
the story of Bambi's father.

misery is:

your beautiful blonde neighbor
coming over to visit with a bottle of booze
ten minutes after you've taken
two sleeping pills.

misery is.

wearing a peek-a-boo dress to a party
and getting more boos than peeks.

misery is:

spending weeks on a diet so you can
look good in a bathing suit,
going for a swim, and having
the life guard shout, "Whale Ho!"

misery is:

having your wife scream so loud that she wants to live in a more expensive apartment that your landlord comes up and raises the rent.